Space

Sue Becklake
Consultant: Peter Bond

M i L e s
K e L L y
PUBLISHING

First published in 2004 by
Miles Kelly Publishing Ltd
Bardfield Centre, Great Bardfield, Essex, CM7 4SL

Copyright © Miles Kelly Publishing Ltd 2004
2 4 6 8 10 9 7 5 3 1

Some material in this book can also be found in
100 Things You Should Know About Space

Editorial Director: Anne Marshall

Editors: Nicola Sail, Amanda Learmonth

Assistant Editor: Nicola Jessop

Design: Maya Currell

British Library Cataloguing-in-Publication Data
A catalogue record for this book is available from the British Library

ISBN 1-84236-230-5

Printed in Singapore

ACKNOWLEDGEMENTS

The publishers would like to thank the following artists
who have contributed to this book:

Kuo Kang Chen, Alan Hancocks, Janos Marffy,
Martin Sanders, Mike Saunders, Rudi Vizi

Computer-generated cartoons by James Evans

Contents

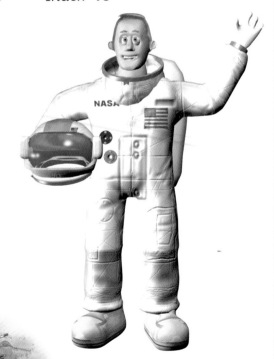

Space is everywhere!

Space is all around the Earth, high above the air. Here on the Earth's surface we are surrounded by air. If you go upwards, up a mountain or in an aircraft, air grows thinner until there is none at all. This is where space begins.

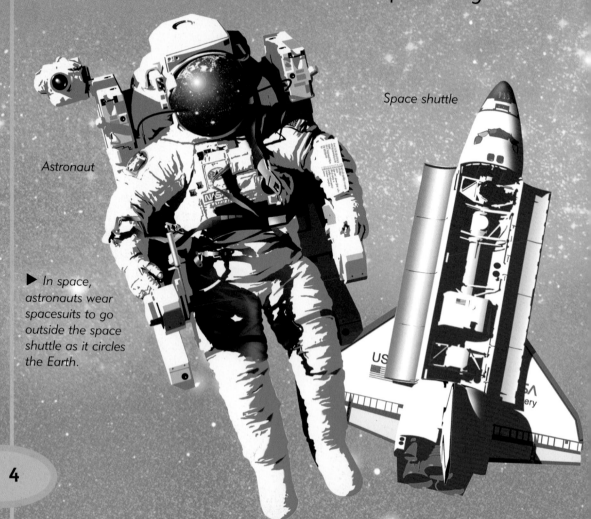

Space shuttle

Astronaut

▶ In space, astronauts wear spacesuits to go outside the space shuttle as it circles the Earth.

Earth

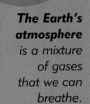

The Earth's atmosphere is a mixture of gases that we can breathe.

The surface of the Earth is made up of land masses and sea.

Astronauts are people who travel in space.

◀ Space itself is mostly empty, but there are many exciting things out there, such as planets, stars and galaxies.

Our life-giving Sun

The Sun is our nearest star. It does not look like other stars because it is much closer to us. Most stars are so far away, they look like points of light in the sky. The Sun is not solid like the Earth, but is a giant ball of superhot gases. These gases are very hot and glow like bonfire flames.

Prominence (huge loop of gas thrown out into space)

▶ The Sun's hot, glowing gas is always on the move, bubbling up to the surface and sinking back down again.

Sunspot

Solar flare

▶ Every so often, the Sun, Moon and Earth line up in space so that the Moon is directly between the Earth and Sun. This stops sunlight from reaching a small area on Earth. The area grows dark and cold, as if night has come early. We call this an eclipse.

Sun

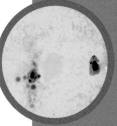

Solar flares are explosions of energy that shoot out from the Sun.

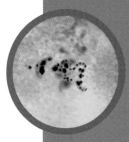

Sunspots are massive, cooler spots on the Sun's surface.

Shadow of the eclipse

Moon

Earth

Andy's fun facts!

The surface of the Sun is nearly 60 times hotter than boiling water. It is so hot it would melt a spacecraft flying near it.

The planet family

The Sun is surrounded by a family of circling planets called the Solar System. This family is held together by an invisible force called gravity, which pulls things towards each other. It is the same force that pulls us to the ground and stops us floating away. The Sun's gravity pulls on the planets and keeps them travelling around it.

Uranus

Neptune

Saturn

Pluto

Jupiter

Moon

Mercury

Earth

Mars

Venus

Sun

Some planets have rings made up of ice, dust and rocks.

From space, we can see the swirling atmospheres of the planets.

Andy's fun facts!

If the Sun was the size of a large beach ball, the Earth would be as small as a pea, and the Moon would look like a pinhead.

▲ The nine planets are all different. Mercury, nearest the Sun, is small and hot. Then Venus, Earth and Mars are rocky and cooler. Beyond them Jupiter, Saturn, Uranus and Neptune are large and cold, while Pluto is tiny and icy.

Earth – our home

The planet we live on is Earth.
It is a round ball of rock. On the outside where we live, the rock is hard and solid. But deep below our feet, inside the Earth, the rock is hot enough to melt. Sometimes this hot rock showers out of an erupting volcano.

Crust

Mantle

Outer core

Inner core

Andy's fun facts!

The Moon has no air or water. When astronauts went to the Moon they had to take air with them in their spacecraft and spacesuits.

▲ If you could look inside the Earth this is what you would see. It has lots of layers like an onion.

▼ The Moon is nearer to the Earth than any other object in space. The Moon travels around the Earth, taking one month to complete its journey.

Craters are scars left by space rocks that hit the Moon's surface.

The inner core, at the centre of the Earth, is made of iron.

The crust is the thin surface layer we live on.

▼ Over a month, the Moon changes from a thin crescent shape to a round shape. This is because sunlight is reflected by the Moon. We see the full Moon when the sunlit side faces the Earth. We see a crescent Moon when the sunlit side is facing away from us.

Crescent Moon

First quarter Moon

Gibbous Moon

Full Moon

11

Earth's neighbours

Venus and Mars are the nearest planets to the Earth. Venus is closer to the Sun than the Earth while Mars is farther away. Each takes a different amount of time to circle the Sun. We call this its year. A year on Venus is 225 days, on Earth 365 days and on Mars 687 days.

◀ There are plans to send astronauts to Mars but the journey would take six months or more.

Olympus Mons is the biggest volcano on Mars.

Valles Marineris is an enormous valley that cuts across Mars.

◀ From space, all we can see of Venus are the tops of its clouds.

The clouds on Venus race around the planet in just four days.

Planet spotting

See if you can spot Venus in the night sky. It is often the first bright star to appear in the evening, just above where the Sun has set. Because of this we sometimes call it the evening star.

13

Tiny planets

Pluto is the smallest planet – smaller than our Moon. It is so tiny and far away that it was not discovered until 1930. Mercury looks like our Moon. It is a round, cratered ball of rock. It has no atmosphere, so the sunny side is boiling hot, while the night side is freezing cold.

▶ *If you were on Pluto, its moon, Charon, would look much larger than our moon does, because Charon is very close to Pluto.*

Make craters

You will need:

• flour • baking tray • a marble or a stone

1. Spread some flour about 2 centimetres deep in a baking tray and smooth over the surface.
2. Drop a marble or a small round stone onto the flour and see the saucer-shaped crater that it makes.

Pluto's moon, Charon, was only discovered in 1976.

▼ Mercury has many craters. This shows how often it was hit by space rocks. One was so large it shattered rocks on the other side of the planet.

The cratered surface of Pluto is covered in solid ice.

The Sun looks huge as it rises on Mercury.

Massive planets

Jupiter is the biggest planet, more massive than all the other planets in the Solar System put together. It is 11 times as wide as the Earth although it is still much smaller than the Sun. Saturn, the next largest planet, is more than nine times as wide as the Earth.

▼▶Jupiter and Saturn are both gas giants. They have no solid surface and all that you can see are the tops of their clouds. Beneath the clouds, the planets are made mostly of gas (like air) and liquid (like water).

Andy's fun facts!

Saturn is the lightest planet in the Solar System. If there was a large enough sea, it would float like a cork.

▼ Jupiter's fast winds blow the cloud into coloured bands around the planet.

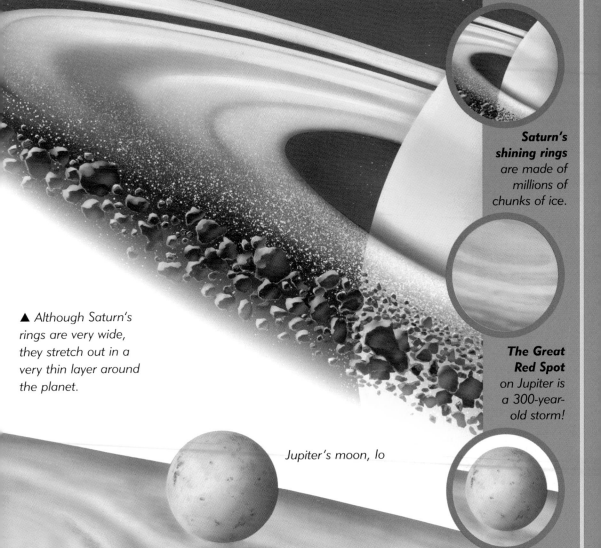

Saturn's shining rings are made of millions of chunks of ice.

▲ Although Saturn's rings are very wide, they stretch out in a very thin layer around the planet.

The Great Red Spot on Jupiter is a 300-year-old storm!

Jupiter's moon, Io

Io has many active volcanoes that change its surface.

17

Far, far away

Uranus and Neptune are gas giants like Jupiter and Saturn. They are the next two planets beyond Saturn but much smaller – less than half as wide. They too have no hard surface. Their cloud tops make Uranus and Neptune look blue.

▶ Like all the gas giant planets, Neptune is surrounded by rings

Neptune

st planets spin upright like a
ut Uranus spins on its side.
have been knocked over
something crashed into
ons of years ago.

Neptune's rings are thinner and darker than Saturn's.

Uranus

Neptune's bright blue clouds make the whole planet look blue.

Test your memory!

1. How many days are there in a year on Earth?
2. Which is the biggest planet in our Solar System?
3. Which is Earth's nearest star?
4. How many planets are there in our Solar System?

1. 365 **2.** Jupiter **3.** the Sun **4.** nine

Uranus is very cold, being so far from the Sun.

Space snowball

A comet is often called a dirty snowball because it is made of dust and ice mixed together. Dust and gas stream away from the comet forming a huge, glowing tail. There may be billions of comets at the edge of the Solar System. They circle the Sun far beyond Pluto.

▲ *The solid part of a comet is hidden inside a huge, glowing cloud that stretches into a long tail.*

▼ Some comets loop around the Sun, then return to where they came from. Others come back to the Sun regularly, such as Halley's comet, which returns every 76 years.

Shooting stars are burning meteors (rocks) flying through space.

Asteroids are chunks of rock that failed to stick to each other to make a planet.

Comet tails always point away from the Sun.

Test your memory!

1. Which planet spins on its side?
2. What colour are Neptune's clouds?
3. On which planet would you find the volcano, Olympus Mons?

1. Uranus 2. blue 3. Mars

Birth of a star

A star is born in clouds of dust and gas called a nebula. Astronomers (scientists who study the stars) can see these clouds as shining patches in the night sky, or dark patches against the distant stars. These clouds shrink as gravity pulls the dust and gas together. At the centre, the gas gets hotter until a new star is born.

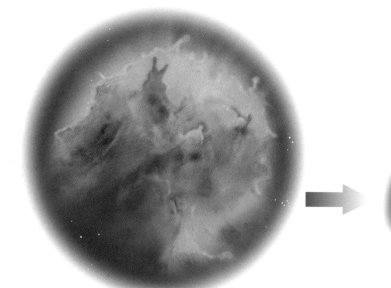

1. Clumps of gas in this nebula start to shrink into tight round balls that will become stars.

2. The gas spirals as it is pulled inwards. Any leftover gas and dust may form planets around the new star.

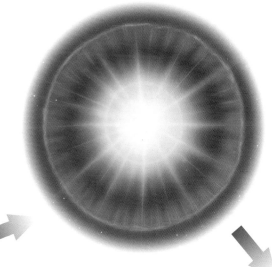

3. Deep in its centre, the new star starts making energy, but it is still hidden by the cloud of dust and gas.

Large white stars make energy very fast and burn brightly.

Small red stars are cooler and shine less brightly.

4. The dust and gas are blown away and we can see the star shining. Maybe it has a family of planets like the Sun.

Our Sun is a star that is about halfway through its ten billion-year-life.

Test your memory!

1. Does a comet's tail always point towards or away from the Sun?
2. Asteroids are chunks of what?
3. Which comet passes Earth every 76 years?

1. away from the Sun
2. rock 3. Halley's comet

So many galaxies

The Sun is part of a huge family of stars called the Milky Way galaxy. There are billions of other stars in our galaxy, as many as the grains of sand on a beach. There are also billions of galaxies outside the Milky Way. Some are larger and some are smaller, but all have more stars than you can count.

Andy's fun facts!

If you could fit the Milky Way onto these two pages, the Sun would be so tiny, you could not see it.

NASA

▼ *Seen from the outside, our galaxy, the Milky Way, would look like this. We call it the Milky Way because it looks like a very faint band of light in the night sky, as though someone has spilt some milk across space.*

***Irregular galaxies** have no particular shape.*

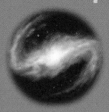

***Spiral galaxies** have arms made of bright stars.*

***Galaxies** that are very close pull each other out of shape.*

25

Exploring the sky

People have imagined they can see the outlines of people and animals in star patterns in the sky. These patterns are called constellations. Astronomers named the constellations to help them find their way around the skies.

Scorpion

Great Dog

Southern Cross

◀ If you live south of the Equator (the imaginary line through the centre of the Earth), these are the constellations that you can see at night.

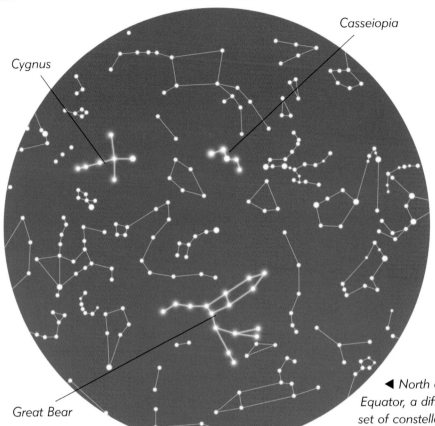

Casseiopia

Cygnus

Great Bear

◄ North of the Equator, a different set of constellations can be seen.

The Scorpion is so-called because it looks like a scorpion.

The Great Bear is one of the best-known star formations.

The Southern Cross can be used as a compass.

Moon-watch

You will need:

- binoculars

On a clear night look at the Moon through binoculars, holding them very steady. You will be able to see the round shapes of craters. Binoculars are really two telescopes, one for each eye, and they make the Moon look bigger so you can see more detail.

27

Launching into space

To blast into space, a rocket has to travel nearly 40 times faster than a jumbo jet.
If it goes any slower, gravity pulls it back to Earth. Rockets are powered by burning fuel, which makes hot gases. These gases rush out of the engines, shooting the rocket forwards.

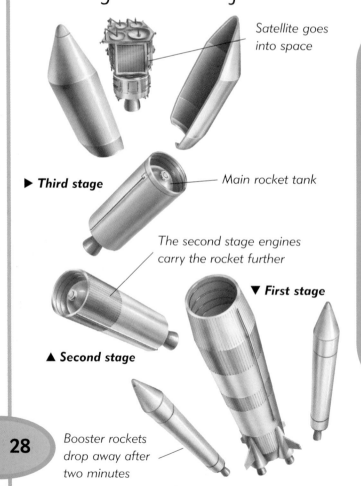

Satellite goes into space

▶ **Third stage**

Main rocket tank

The second stage engines carry the rocket further

▼ **First stage**

▲ **Second stage**

Booster rockets drop away after two minutes

Rocket power

You will need:

• *balloon*

If you blow up a balloon and let it go, the balloon shoots off across the room. The air inside the balloon has rushed out, pushing the balloon away in the opposite direction. A rocket blasting into space works in a similar way.

◀ *A single rocket is not powerful enough to launch a spacecraft or satellite into space, so rockets have two or three stages.*

◄ The space shuttle takes off from Earth as a rocket.

Booster rocket

Space shuttle

USA

UNITED STATES

Booster rockets give extra speed to a spacecraft.

The main rocket tank drops away after six minutes.

Satellites need rockets to launch them into space.

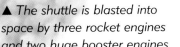

▲ The shuttle is blasted into space by three rocket engines and two huge booster engines.

29

Life in space

Space is a dangerous place for astronauts.
It can be boiling hot in the sunshine or freezing
cold in the Earth's shadow. There is also radiation
(rays of energy) from the Sun. Dust, rocks and bits
from other rockets speed through space at such
speed, they could easily make a small hole in
a spacecraft, letting the air leak out.

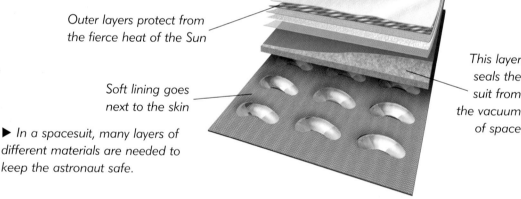

Outer layers protect from
the fierce heat of the Sun

This layer
seals the
suit from
the vacuum
of space

Soft lining goes
next to the skin

▶ In a spacesuit, many layers of
different materials are needed to
keep the astronaut safe.

Space meals

You will need:

• dried noodles

Ask an adult to help you. Buy a dried snack such as
noodles, that just needs water added. This is the kind
of food astronauts eat. Most of their meals are dried
so they are not too heavy to launch into space.

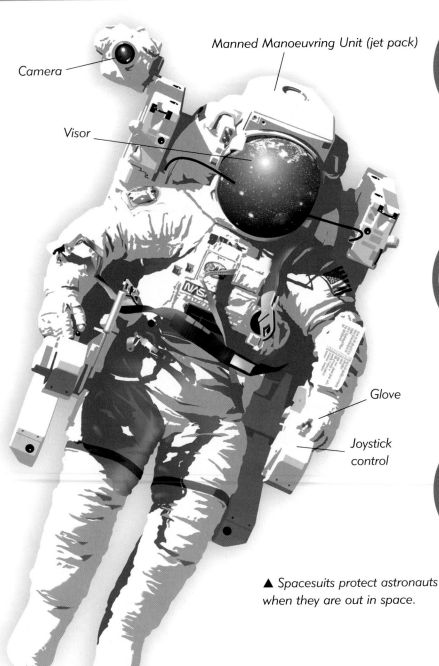

Camera

Manned Manoeuvring Unit (jet pack)

Visor

NASA

Glove

Joystick
control

▲ Spacesuits protect astronauts
when they are out in space.

The visor
protects the
astronaut's
face from
the sunlight.

**The joystick
control** lets
the astronaut
move around
in space.

**Tubes of
water** under
the spacesuit
carry away
heat.

31

At home in space

A space station is a home in space for astronauts and cosmonauts (Russian astronauts). It has a kitchen for making meals, cabins with sleeping bags, toilets, washbasins and sometimes showers. The space station has places to work and controls where astronauts can check that everything is working properly.

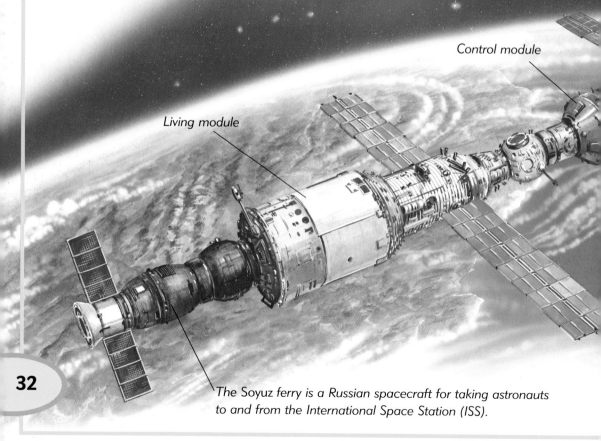

Control module

Living module

The Soyuz ferry is a Russian spacecraft for taking astronauts to and from the International Space Station (ISS).

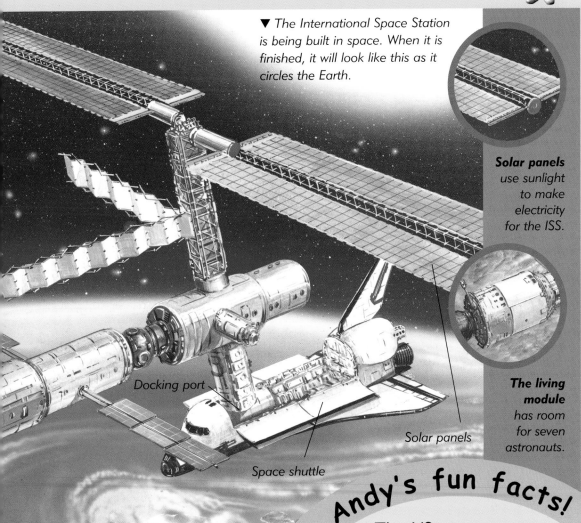

▼ The International Space Station is being built in space. When it is finished, it will look like this as it circles the Earth.

Solar panels use sunlight to make electricity for the ISS.

The living module has room for seven astronauts.

Docking port

Solar panels

Space shuttle

▲ Sixteen countries are helping to build the International Space Station, including the US, Russia, Japan, Canada, Brazil and 11 European countries.

Andy's fun facts!

The US space station Skylab, launched in 1973, fell back to Earth in 1979. Most of it landed in the ocean but some pieces hit Australia!

Exploring with robots

Robot spacecraft called probes have explored all the planets except Pluto. Probes travel in space to take close-up pictures and measurements. They send the information back to scientists on Earth. Some probes circle planets taking pictures. For a close-up look, a probe can land on the surface.

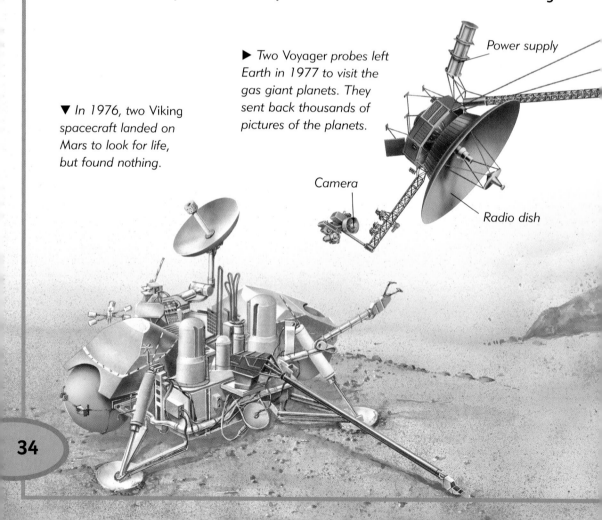

▶ Two Voyager probes left Earth in 1977 to visit the gas giant planets. They sent back thousands of pictures of the planets.

▼ In 1976, two Viking spacecraft landed on Mars to look for life, but found nothing.

Power supply

Camera

Radio dish

Test your memory!

1. What is the name of the galaxy we live in?

2. What do we call a pattern of stars?

3. How much faster than a jumbo jet does a rocket need to travel to get into space?

4. What kind of rockets give extra speed to a space shuttle taking off?

3. 40 times 4. booster rockets
1. the Milky Way 2. constellation

Probes have their own power supply to explore the planets.

▼ Sojourner was like a remote control car with six wheels. It spent three months on Mars, testing the soil and rocks to find out what they were made of.

Cameras on a probe take detailed pictures of a planet.

The radio dish sends messages back to Earth.

Space spies

Hundreds of satellites circle the Earth in space. They are used for communication, checking the weather, making maps and finding out more about space. They are launched into space by rockets and may stay there for ten years or more.

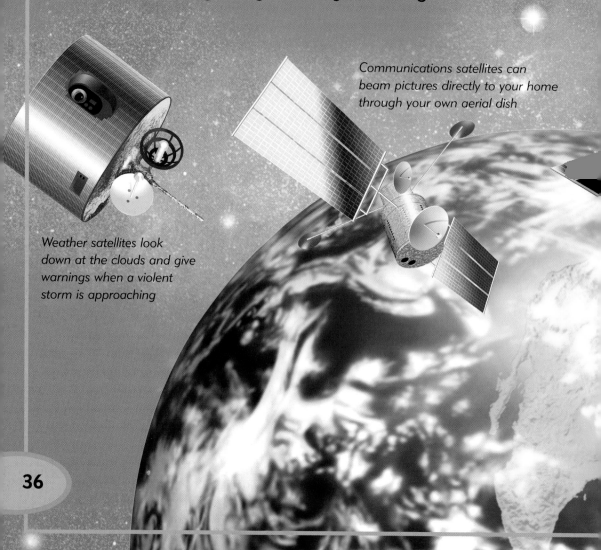

Communications satellites can beam pictures directly to your home through your own aerial dish

Weather satellites look down at the clouds and give warnings when a violent storm is approaching

▼ *Different satellites each have their own job to do, looking at the Earth, or the weather, or out into space.*

Special satellite telescopes let astronomers look far out into the Universe and discover what is out there

Earth-watching satellites look out for pollution, such as dirty air over cities

Satellites *can spot icebergs that may be a danger to ships.*

Pictures of the Earth *can help make accurate maps.*

Andy's fun facts!

Spy satellites circling the Earth take pictures of secret locations and listen to secret radio messages from military ships or aircraft.

Off to the Moon

The first men landed on the Moon in 1969. They were three astronauts from the US *Apollo 11* mission. Neil Armstrong was the first person to set foot on the Moon. Only five other *Apollo* missions have landed on the Moon since then.

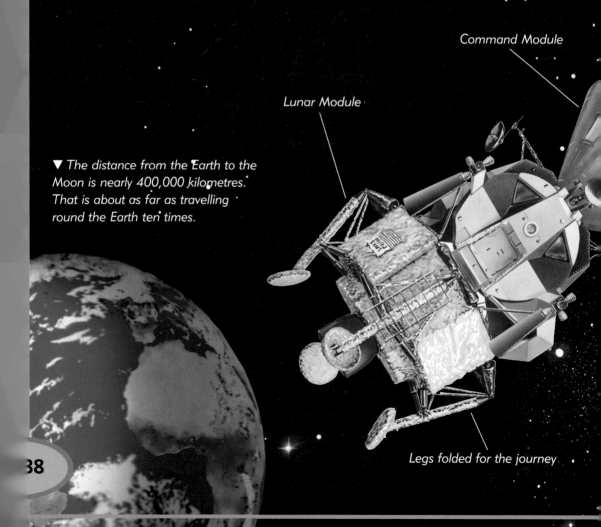

Command Module

Lunar Module

▼ The distance from the Earth to the Moon is nearly 400,000 kilometres. That is about as far as travelling round the Earth ten times.

Legs folded for the journey

The Lunar Module took two astronauts to the Moon's surface.

The Command Module was the same size as a car.

The longest time spent on the Moon was three days.

Main engine

Service Module with fuel and air supplies

▲ The Lunar and Command Modules travelled to the Moon fixed together, then separated for the Moon landing.

39

Index